MY TALEEM

MY THIRTY days OF  RAMADAN activity JOURNAL

This journal belongs to:

MY TALEEM

RAMADAN

IN THE SPOTLIGHT!

UPLOAD A SNAP OF YOUR DAILY RAMADAN ACTIVITIES FOR A CHANCE TO BE FEATURED ON OUR INSTAGRAM PAGE.

Don't forget to tag us!

⬚ mytaleem

*CHILDREN UNDER THE AGE OF 16 MUST SEEK PARENTAL CONSENT.
*PLEASE VISIT OUR INSTAGRAM PAGE TO VIEW OUR REFERENCE LIST FOR ISLAMIC AUTHENTICITY.

CONTENTS PAGE

PUBLISHED BY MY TALEEM LTD
WWW.MYTALEEM.CO.UK

MY TALEEM

PUBLISHED BY MY TALEEM 2021
TEXT COPYRIGHT Ⓒ FARHANA ISLAM, 2021
MORAL RIGHTS ASSERTED.

The Hijri Calendar

Have you ever wondered why Ramadan and Eid are brought forward every year?

The solar calendar is something we're all very familiar with, but did you know that Islam follows the lunar calendar? This means that the beginning of every month is identified by the appearance of a new crescent moon. This happens every 29 or 30 days. The biggest difference between the two calendars is that the lunar calendar is around 11 days shorter than the solar calendar. You may have also heard people describe the Islamic calendar as the 'Hijri' calendar. That's because the first year of the Islamic calendar was the year the hijra took place. That was when Prophet Muhammad (SAW) migrated from Makkah to Madinah.

Task: Observe the Ramadan moon across this holy month and complete the lunar chart below.

day 1	day 2	day 3	day 4	day 5	day 6
day 7	day 8	day 9	day 10	day 11	day 12
day 13	day 14	day 15	day 16	day 17	day 18
day 19	day 20	day 21	day 22	day 23	day 24
day 25	day 26	day 27	day 28	day 29	day 30

Remembering Allah (SWT)

There are so many ways to remember and praise Allah (SWT), thousands, in fact... maybe even millions!

You do it EVERY SINGLE DAY. Probably without even realising. Some of the Arabic expressions we use to praise Allah (SWT) are taken directly from the Quran and others are used for the remembrance of Him.

BISMILLAH!

JAZAKALLAH KHAIR

IN SHA ALLAH

MA SHAA' ALLAH TABAARAK ALLAH

It's VERY important to keep these expressions locked in our brain and get into a habit of using them EVERY DAY.

Task: Here are just a few examples of the common phrases you may hear at home. Can you match each Arabic expression to its meaning and use?

ARABIC EXPRESSION	GENERAL TRANSLATION	WHEN COULD YOU USE IT?	
			Subhan'Allah
	If Allah (SWT) wills	When you have the intention to do something	Fisabillah
	Glory to Allah (SWT)	When something or someone is being praised	Ma shaa' Allah Tabaarak Allah
	As Allah (SWT) wills, blessed is He	When showing appreciation for the blessings of Allah (SWT)	In sha Allah
	I seek Allah's (SWT) forgiveness	When you want to say sorry to Allah (SWT)	Astagfirullah
	For the sake of Allah (SWT)	When giving charity	

6

Prophets in Islam

Did you know that every prophet is a Nabi, but not every Nabi is a Rasool AKA a Messenger?

A Rasool delivers a new message, a new law or a new book directly from Allah (SWT), like Prophets Muhammad (SAW), Musa (AS) and Nuh (AS). A Nabi is a little different, they spread messages from Allah (SWT) too, but the messages they spread were first revealed to the Rasool that came before them. Although we don't know EXACTLY how many prophets Allah (SWT) sent down to mankind, 25 of them are mentioned by name in the Quran.

Task: Can you find the 25 prophets mentioned in the Quran in the word search below?

```
M A D A R T N D P A S D F I
U E A X Y U Y U S U F G S B
H W H G I O K W H J H A H R
A L Y A S A L A Z X C V U A
M Z U Y Y T S D R Y N B A H
M A I S U L A Y M A N M I I
A K O P N S L T E Q W Q B M
D A A H U D E D F U G T N H
N R I T S E H S D B B U U J
B I S L R W Q Z X C V L R K
V Y M Y Y A H Y A A C N A L
C A A U I A L F I K L U H D
A H I D R I S D I S H A Q M
I O L E E M U S A B A Y U B
```

SULAYMAN	AYUB	LUT	DHUL KIFL	IDRIS
IBRAHIM	NUH	AL YASA	ISA	SHUAIB
YAQUB	YAHYA	ISMAIL	YUSUF	HARUN
ILYAS	YUNUS	HUD	MUSA	ISHAQ
ADAM	MUHAMMAD	SALEH	DAWUD	ZAKARIYAH

My Ibadah Checklist

Did you know that ibadah isn't just salah, dhikr, fasting and reading Quran?

YES, of course all of these are REALLY important, but if we have the right intentions, the things we do every day can be a form of ibadah too. Things like sleeping, cooking, eating, cleaning and even bathing are all things Allah (SWT) will reward us for.

Allah (SWT) LOVES to give rewards to those that worship Him, so remember to start every action with a sincere intention and...

'BISMILLAH HIR RAHMAN NIR RAHIM'

In the name of Allah, the Most Gracious, the Most Merciful.

Task: Let's make an ibadah checklist. Plan things to do across the day that you know will make Allah (SWT) happy. Here are some ideas to help you get started!

IBADAH CHECKLIST

I listened to a story about one of the prophets in Islam. ✓

I took care of my body by doing some exercise. ✓

I donated something to charity. ✓

I fed an animal. ✓

I recited some dhikr across the day. ✓

I helped my family set the table for iftar. ✓

I helped clean the dishes after iftar. ✓

I performed salah with somebody else. ✓

I performed wudu before going to bed. ✓

Allah's (SWT) Ninety Nine Names

'And to Allah (SWT) belong the best names, so call on Him by them.'
- Surah Al A'raf 7:180

Did you know that Prophet Muhammad (SAW) said that whoever knows the 99 names of Allah (SWT) will enter Jannah (Bukhari and Muslim)? Allah (SWT) has made it so easy for us to please Him!

How many words do you know? Probably hundreds, if not thousands, right? So taking the time to learn and understand His 99 names is definitely something we can do if we set our minds to it. Out of ALL of the names Allah (SWT) could have chosen, He has chosen to reveal THESE names to us because they help us get closer to Him.

Think about it, what do we need to survive? Food? Warmth? Sustenance? By revealing 'Ar Razzaaq, Allah (SWT) is reminding us that He is The Provider. We also need protection to feel safe. By revealing 'Al Hafiz', Allah (SWT) is reminding us that He is The Guardian. Love is VERY important too. By revealing 'Al Wadud', Allah (SWT) is reminding us that He is The Most Loving.

Try and remember to use Allah's (SWT) names when you're making dua for something, or before you thank Allah (SWT) for something.
Here is a dua you can make right now!

'Allah (SW). You are Ar Raqeeb. You are The Watchful. Please watch over me and my family.'

Task: Turn the page to find a table with a handful of Allah's (SWT) 99 names recorded on. Use the internet, your grown ups or books to help record the meaning of each name.

One has been done for you.

Allah's (SWT) Name	Meaning
Al Malik	The Ultimate Sovereign and King
Al Quddus	
Al Ghaffar	
Al Mu'min	
Al Hakeem	
Al Kareem	
Al Muqeet	
Al Hafiz	
Ash Shakur	
Al Alim	
Al Wahhab	
As Sabur	

Prayer Mats

Did you know that the whole, ENTIRE earth is a mosque/masjid for us?

It's really easy to get into a habit of praying in the same place every day, but why not shake things up a bit? EVERY SINGLE place in which you offer your salah will speak for you on the Day of Judgement.

Task: Plan your salah. Choose a different space to pray in - can you pray in at least three different places today? i.e bedroom, living room, garden, mosque etc.

Did you know that using a prayer mat when performing salah is a sunnah? It was reported that Prophet Muhammad (SAW) used a khumrah (a small mat made from palm leaves) so that he remained in a state of purity when prostrating. The khumrah acted as a shield between him and any dirt on the ground. It's no wonder that cleanliness is such a big part of our iman (faith). Of course, that doesn't mean your salah won't count if you don't use one, just make extra sure that the ground you prostrate on is clean!

Have a look at the prayer mats in your home. What do you notice?

They sometimes have floral patterns, geometric designs or thread work to illustrate the Kaabah or a mosque.

Task: Design your own prayer mat.

Prophet Nuh (AS)

One thousand years after Prophet Adam (AS), Allah (SWT) sent Prophet Nuh (AS) down to Earth.

Very few believed in Allah (SWT) and instead, the people chose to worship idols.

Prophet Nuh (AS), however, was NOT one of them.

He was a blessed man with incredible patience.

It was for this reason Prophet Nuh (AS) was chosen by Allah (SWT) to guide the people back to Him.

You've probably guessed it, this job came with GREAT difficulty.

Prophet Nuh (AS) tried ever so hard to guide the people, but they just wouldn't listen, no matter how beautiful and eloquent in speech he was.

Prophet Nuh (AS) told the people to fear Allah (SWT).

He shouted it for everybody to hear.

He told them all that he knew.

He told them about Allah's (SWT) beautiful creations, the sun, the moon, the shimmering stars and the night sky.

He told them about the mountains, the deserts, the rivers, the trees and everything that lives and breathes. But still they did not listen.

Prophet Nuh (AS) strived and he strived, but the people had enough. They threatened to hurt him and they laughed and they mocked him.

He strived for 950 years, all for the sake of Allah (SWT).

Prophet Nuh (AS) was truly blessed. Allah (SWT) loved him very much and of course He had a plan. One night, Allah (SWT) spoke to Prophet Nuh (AS) and asked him to plant some trees.

Day seven (cont)

He did what was asked of him and years passed by. Prophet Nuh (AS) never lost faith in his Lord. After a while, Allah (SWT) spoke to Prophet Nuh (AS) once more. Allah (SWT) told him to build a big boat with the trees he had planted. Prophet Nuh (AS) was no carpenter and the people mocked him some more. What use was a boat in the middle of a desert? But Prophet Nuh's (AS) faith was strong. He worked tirelessly all day and all night. The people continued to mock, but it didn't matter. Even the ANGELS came down to help Prophet Nuh (AS).

Some time passed.

And then came the flood.

By the will of Allah (SWT), the boat was ready. Every believer and every animal climbed aboard, two by two.

The rain poured and it poured.

It plummeted down.

THERE WAS NO END IN SIGHT!

The sun disappeared and darkness swallowed the light. The storm was FEROCIOUS and swept up the land and homes disappeared with Allah's (SWT) command. Nowhere was safe and nowhere was calm...

...except a big boat that would come to no harm.

Then, by Allah's (SWT) command, the rain came to a HALT.

The land became clear and the clouds disappeared.

The believers were grateful; they prostrated and prayed!

They trusted their Lord and never once strayed.

Day seven (cont)

1) How many years after Prophet Adam (AS) did Allah (SWT) send Prophet Nuh (AS)?

2) What did the people worship instead of Allah (SWT)?

3) Find and copy a reason why Allah (SWT) might have chosen Prophet Nuh (AS) to guide the people.

4) Find and copy two adjectives that describe Prophet Nuh's (AS) speech.

5) Find and copy four of Allah's creations from the text.

6) What does it mean if Prophet Nuh (AS) 'strived'?

7) True or False - Prophet Nuh (AS) struggled to understand why Allah (SWT) had asked him to plant some trees.

8) Explain the feelings and emotions of those that joined Prophet Nuh (AS) on the boat.

Wudu and Purity

Did you know cleanliness and purity is part of your iman (faith)?

IN FACT cleanliness is HALF our faith (Sahih Muslim).
You've probably heard that before but have you ever thought about what it actually means?

How can purity and cleanliness be half of our faith?

Prophet Muhammad (SAW) reportedly said...
THE HEART OF BEING A MUSLIM IS YOUR SALAH.
Lets think about our actions before we pray...

We face the direction of the qiblah at the correct time. We make the intention to pray and for Allah (SWT) to accept it. We pray the way that Prophet Muhammad (SAW) prayed.

IS IT POSSIBLE TO PRAY OUR SALAH WITHOUT WUDU?

Wudu is a ritual act. It's a form of worship that helps us in LOTS of ways. Not only does it physically purify us, it mentally purifies us too. It allows us to get closer to Allah (SWT) and acts as an expiation of sins. That just means wudu helps us to atone, to seek redemption, and to make amends for any sins that we want forgiveness for.

DID YOU KNOW THAT THERE ARE TWO TYPES OF WUDU?

WET ABLUTION

Tap water isn't the only type of water we can use to perform wudu. We can use any water that is pure by nature, such as water from lakes, rivers, seas and waterfalls.

DRY ABLUTION

TAYAMMUM is dry ablution.
If you don't have access to water or you're injured or sick and unable to use water, you should do tayammum. All you need is earth - something that is natural and free of impurities, like dust, dirt or stone.

Task: Research how to perform tayammum (dry ablution) and create a step by step diagram to share with somebody else.

Your Salah

When you learn the importance of salah, you begin to THINK about it more, you begin to CHERISH it more and you begin to LOVE it more.

It is our link to Allah (SWT). It makes us feel closer to Him across the WHOLE day and it's our very own way of PURIFYING our souls. It's the key to TRUE success in this world and the next.

SALAH IS FOOD FOR OUR SOULS.

Did you know that Allah (SWT) originally prescribed FIFTY prayers and not FIVE?

Salah is SO IMPORTANT that it is the SECOND pillar of Islam, straight after the shahada. It's a pretty big deal!

Each salah can be split up into three parts:

FARD PRAYERS

These prayers are for Allah (SWT).

SUNNAH PRAYERS

These prayers are for Prophet Muhammad (SAW).

NAFL PRAYERS

These prayers are for you.

KEY VOCAB FOR SALAH

KEY VOCAB FOR SALAH	MEANING
Intention - Niyyah	...deciding to pray
Takbir	...saying Allahu Akbar
Ruku	...bowing in prayer
Sujood	...prostrating in prayer
Qiyam	...standing in prayer
Tasleem	...saying salam at the end of prayer
Adhan	...main call to prepare for prayer
Iqamah	...the second call to start the prayer

Task: Use what you have read about salah to complete the crossword.

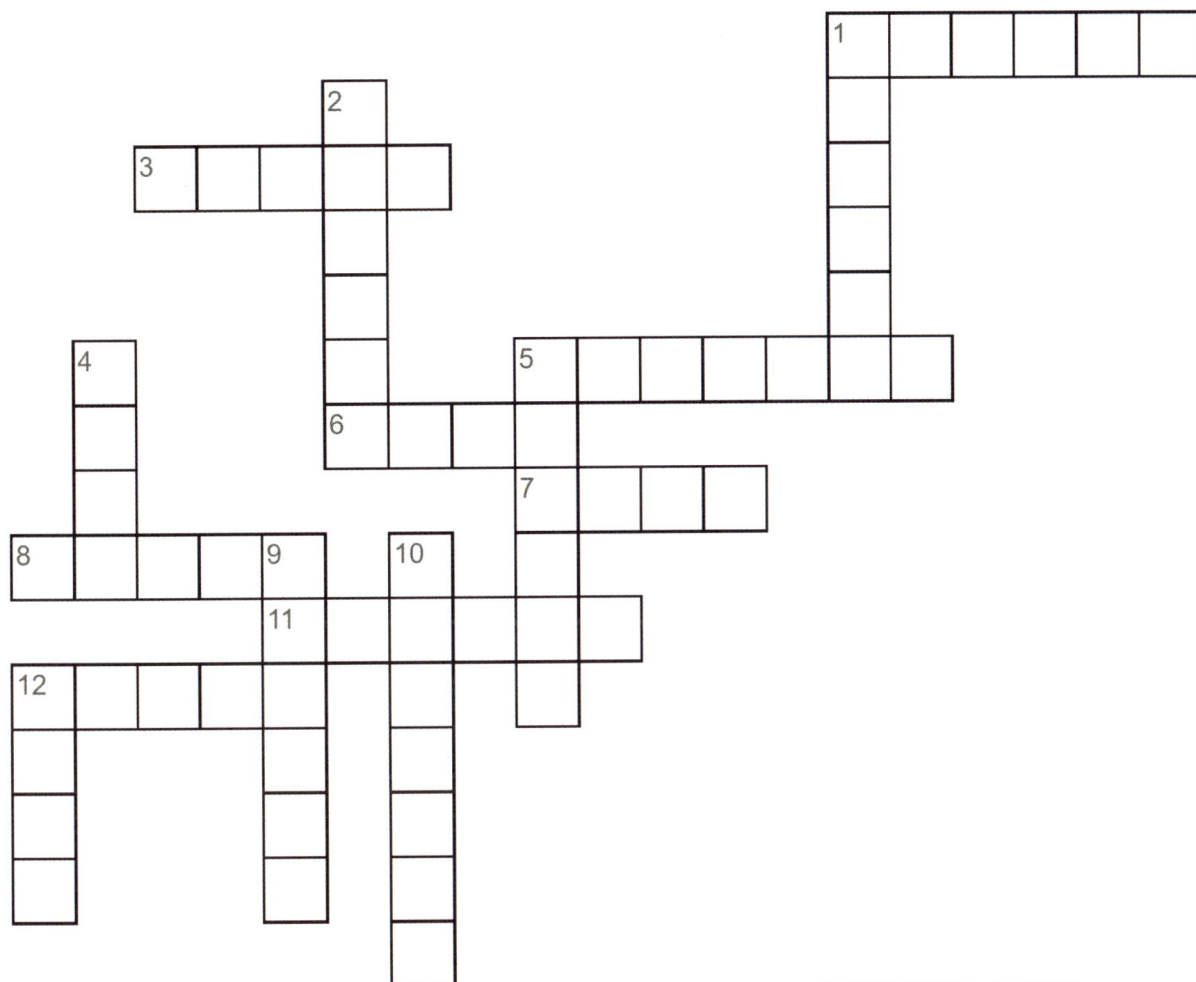

ACROSS

1 Prostrating in salah

3 Standing in salah

5 The first pillar in Islam

6 Bowing in salah

7 Prayers specifically for you in salah

8 The main call to prepare for salah

11 The second call to start salah

12 The number of salah Allah (SWT) originally prescribed

DOWN

1 Salah is the _____ pillar of Islam

2 Saying Allahu Akbar in salah

4 Prayers specifically for Allah (SWT) in salah

5 Prayers specifically for Prophet Muhammad (SAW) in salah

9 The Arabic word for intention

10 Saying salam at the end of salah

12 The number of salah we perform daily

Allah's (SWT) Angels

Allah (SWT) has made lots of different kinds of creatures, all with different purposes.

We can see some of them with our very own eyes, and some of those we can't.

ONE OF THOSE IS AL MALAIKAH... THE ANGELS!

The Angels are made of pure light.

Their job is a pretty important job. It's to do whatever Allah (SWT) tells them. And guess what? They CAN'T disobey Him. Unlike us humans, they have NO choice and NO free will. This also means that angels are unable to commit sin. Just like believing in Allah (SWT) and the prophets in Islam, believing in angels is a huge part of our iman.

According to the Quran and sunnah, angels sometimes take a human form when they come down to Earth. But most of the time, they're incredibly big. MASSIVE in fact. GINORMOUS.

They are NEITHER male nor female and they're very, very beautiful. Their sole purpose is to worship Allah (SWT). They don't even need to take a break to go to the bathroom or eat or drink! Oh, and the rumours are true, they really do have wings. Angel Jibreel apparently has 600 of them!

DID YOU KNOW THAT THE ANGELS GATHER AND LISTEN TO YOU WHEN YOU RECITE WORDS FROM THE QURAN?

That's because Allah (SWT) blessed all of mankind with the virtue of reading Quran, and as much as the angels would like to read and recite, Allah (SWT) honoured the children of Adam (AS) over His angels.

We're not EXACTLY sure how many angels there are, but we do know there are WAY too many to count.

ANGEL JIBREEL
(He receives Allah's (SWT) words and communicates them to His prophets)

ANGEL ISRAFEEL
(He is in charge of blowing the trumpet to mark the Day of Judgement)

ANGEL MIKAIL
(He is in charge of the rainfall that waters the land and helps provide sustenance)

ANGEL AZRAEEL
(He is the angel that collects souls upon death)

ANGEL MUNKAR & NAKEER
(They will question the souls in the grave about their faith and deeds)

ANGEL RAQIB & ATID
(The honourable scribes - They sit on your left and right shoulders and record good/bad deeds)

ANGEL RIDHWAN
(He is known as the Angel of Paradise and he guards the gates of Jannah)

ANGEL MALIK
(He is the guardian angel of Jahannam AKA Hell)

Task: Use the text about Allah's (SWT) angels to help answer the questions.

1. What is the Arabic word for angels? _____

2. What did Allah (SWT) make angels from? _____

3. Name two things angels CAN'T do. _____

_____

4. True or False - Angels are ALWAYS invisible. Explain your answer.

_____

_____

5. How do we know so much about angels? _____

6. True or False - Angels recite the Quran every single night. Explain your answer.

_____

7. Record 5 facts about angels.

_____

_____

_____

_____

_____

Task: Complete the table using what you know about the angels.

	These angels question the souls in the grave.
	These angels are the scribes and record your good and bad deeds.
ANGEL RIDHWAN	
ANGEL MIKAIL	
	This angel receives Allah's (SWT) words and tells them to the prophets.
ANGEL ISRAFEEL	

Surahs in the Quran

Did you know that there are ONE HUNDRED AND FOURTEEN surahs in the Quran?

During Ramadan, Prophet Muhammad (SAW) spent a lot of time in a cave on MOUNT HIRA.

IT WAS IN THIS CAVE THAT HE FOUND PEACE AND QUIET.

It was in this cave he was able to contemplate and ponder ALL things.

It was in this cave Prophet Muhammad (SAW)
received his FIRST revelation.

One night, during the HOLY MONTH of RAMADAN, as commanded by Allah (SWT), angel Jibreel appeared in front of Prophet Muhammad (SAW).

He revealed words from the Quran for the very first time.

Naturally, Prophet Muhammad (SAW) was so shocked and couldn't believe what had just happened that he ran home to the person he knew would comfort him:

his wife, Khadijah (RA).

Prophet Muhammad (SAW) ran to her and cried out...

'ZAMILOONI, DATHIROONI!' - COVER ME, WRAP ME!'

It was in that moment they knew.

He had been chosen by Allah (SWT) to be the LAST and FINAL Messenger of ALL of mankind.

He was the seal of the prophets.

The very best of men.

HE WAS PROPHET MUHAMMAD (SAW).

Task: Gather some research and complete the table by identifying the surah name, its meaning and the surah number.

SURAH	MEANING	SURAH NUMBER
Surah An-Nisa		
Surah Al-Nahl		
	The Cave	18
	The Prophets	21
		24
		29
Surah Al-Najm		
	The Night	
Surah Al-Fil		
		110
	The Daybreak	

Maze to Makkah

'LABBAYK ALLAHUMMA LABBAYK'
HERE I AM, O ALLAH, HERE I AM

Day twelve

Task: Help the pilgrims reach the Kaabah all the way from the airport.

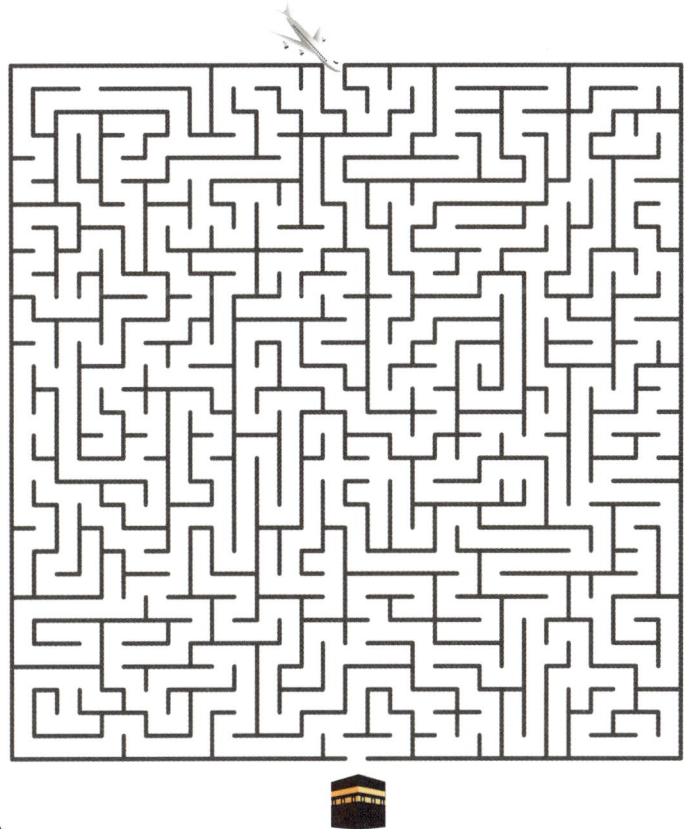

Prophet Muhammad's (SAW) Family Tree

Did you know that Prophet Muhammad (SAW) is a descendant of Prophet Ibrahim (AS)?

Task: Explore Prophet Muhammad's (SAW) family tree. Can you name some of the people that were closest to him?

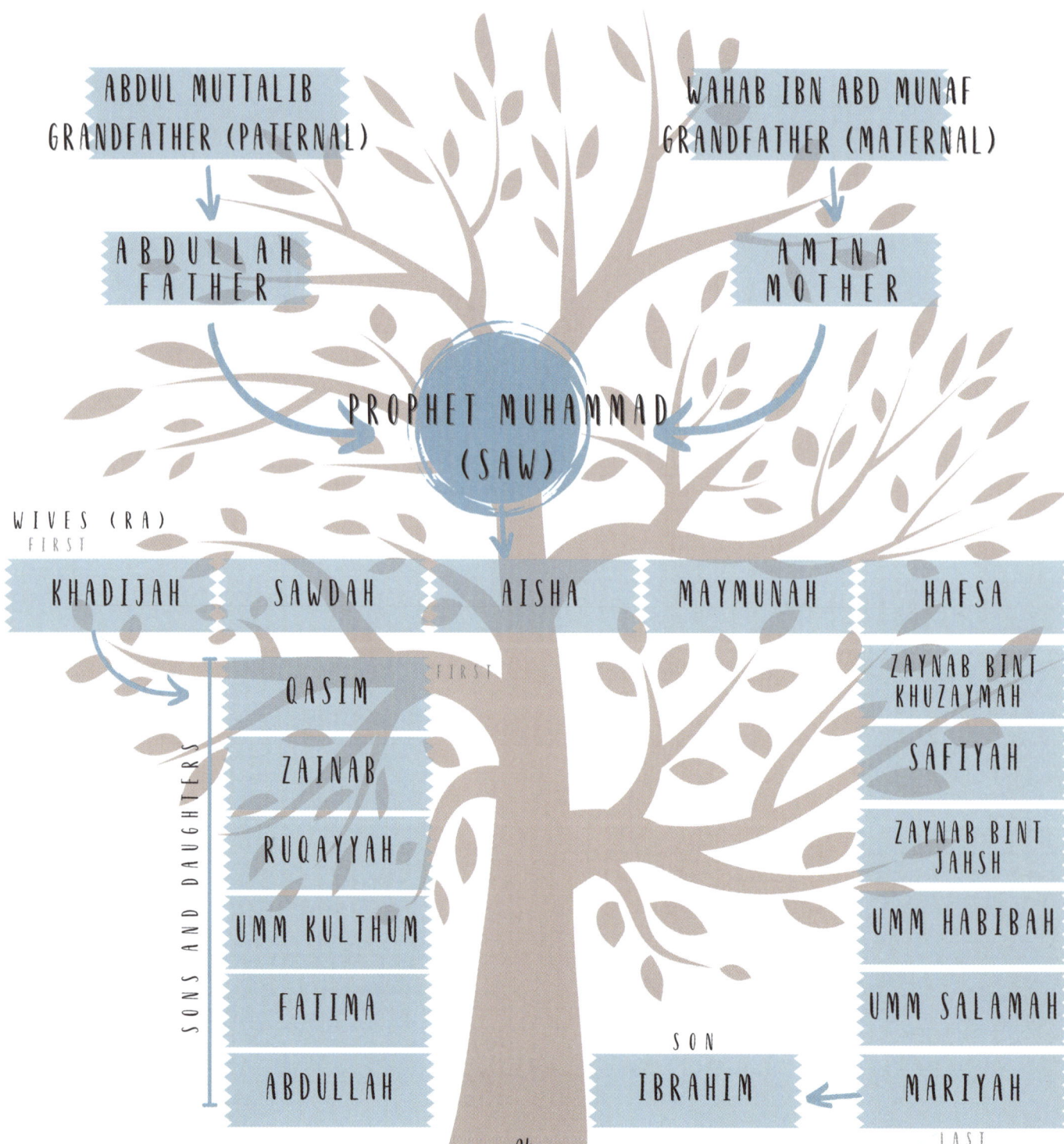

ABDUL MUTTALIB
GRANDFATHER (PATERNAL)

WAHAB IBN ABD MUNAF
GRANDFATHER (MATERNAL)

ABDULLAH
FATHER

AMINA
MOTHER

PROPHET MUHAMMAD (SAW)

WIVES (RA)
FIRST

KHADIJAH   SAWDAH   AISHA   MAYMUNAH   HAFSA

FIRST

SONS AND DAUGHTERS

QASIM

ZAINAB

RUQAYYAH

UMM KULTHUM

FATIMA

ABDULLAH

ZAYNAB BINT KHUZAYMAH

SAFIYAH

ZAYNAB BINT JAHSH

UMM HABIBAH

UMM SALAMAH

MARIYAH

SON
IBRAHIM

LAST

24

Task: Unscramble each word to reveal somebody in Prophet Muhammad's (SAW) family.

M B I R I H A

I F M A T A

I N A Z A B

I M A S Q

S H A A I

S H A F A

A D K I H H J A

M I A N A

B D L A H A U L

Task: Use Prophet Muhammad's (SAW) family tree to answer the questions.

1. Who was Prophet Muhammad's (SAW) first wife? _____

2. What was the name of Prophet Muhammad's (SAW) father? _____

3. Name Prophet Muhammad's (SAW) first born daughter. _____

4. Who was Ibrahim's mother? _____

5. Who is Abdul Muttalib to Prophet Muhammad (SAW)? _____

6. Name Ruqayyah's grandmother. _____

7. Name Umm Kulthum's older brother. _____

8. How many children did Khadijah (RA) and Prophet Muhammad (SAW) have? ____

Day fourteen

Bismillah   salah   Shawwal

Quran   Taraweeh   Muhammad (SAW)

suhoor   Hajj   Laylatul Qadr

sunnah

1) Allah (SWT) has made it obligatory for every Muslim to perform their 5 daily

_____.

2) Before we begin something, we should always say _____.

3) The reward of performing Umrah during Ramadan is the same as _____.

4) The _____ was revealed to Prophet Muhammad (SAW) over 23 years.

5) Prophet _____ is also called Ahmad in the Quran.

6) The month after Ramadan is called _____.

7) There are many blessings for waking up in Ramadan for _____.

8) One of the most exciting things about Ramadan is praying _____ prayers

at the mosque.

9) The 'Night of Power' falls in Ramadan and is called _____.

10) It is a _____ to break your fast with a date, just like the Prophet

Muhammad (SAW) did.

Day fifteen

Crack the Code

Task: Crack the codes to reveal the hidden messages.

A	B	C	D	E	F	G	H	I	J	K	L	M
□	▱	▽	◇	△	○	⬡	✚	⌢	⇨	✛	▭	⬠

N	O	P	Q	R	S	T	U	V	W	X	Y	Z
⬌	⬠	∪	✦	◈	◺	◎	⊠	☽	⊕	⬇	—	☆

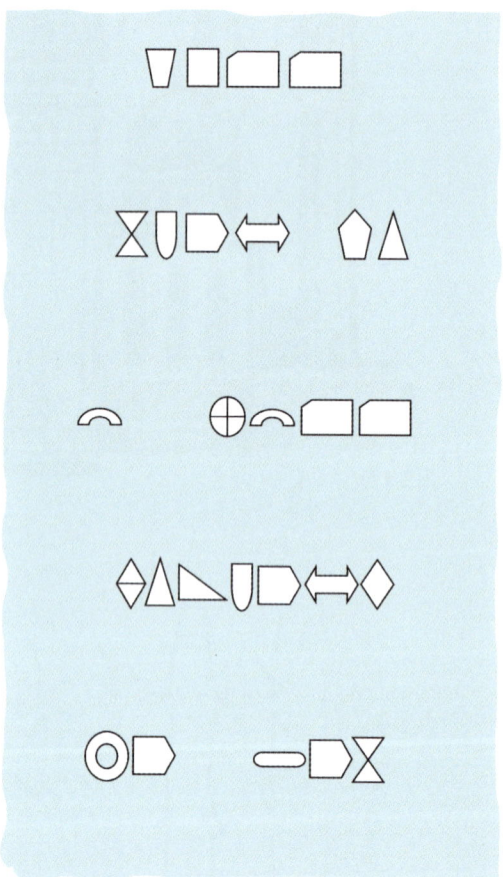

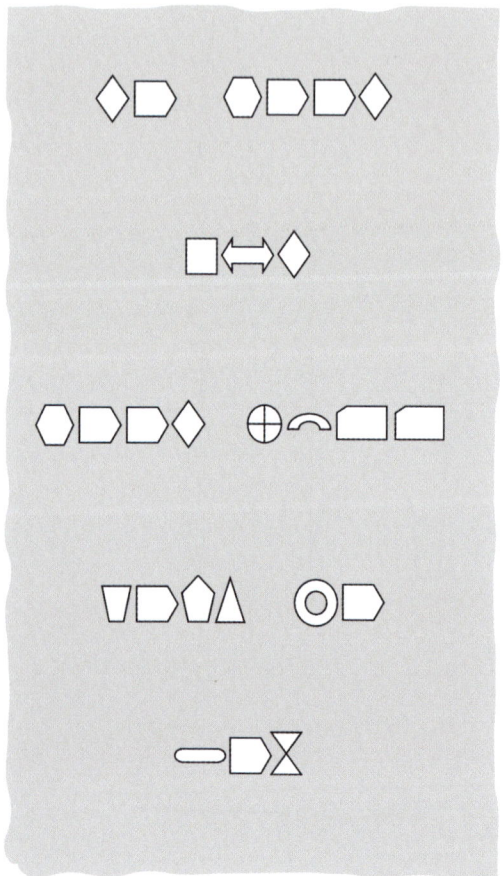

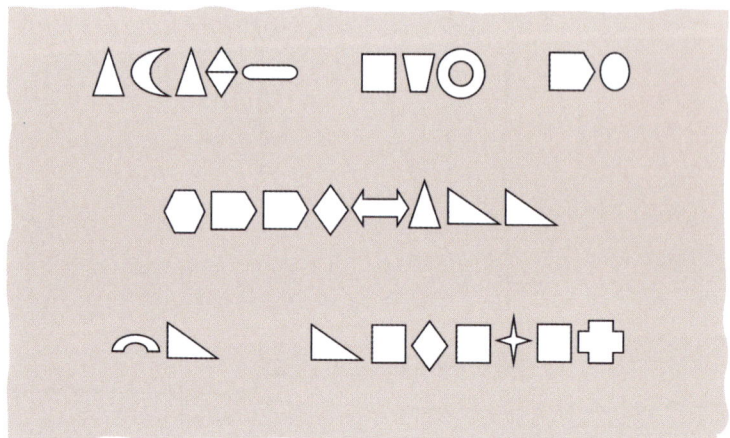

Day seventeen

Saying ALHAMDULLILAH

'IF YOU ARE GRATEFUL, I WILL SURELY GIVE YOU MORE AND MORE.'

(SURAH IBRAHIM 14:7)

There are MILLIONS of reasons to say ALHAMDULLILAH.

Saying ALHAMDULLILAH is not just for our blessings, we should also say ALHAMDULLILAH for the trials we face too. In fact, the greatest blessings come in the form of hardships! During this time of year, it's EXTRA important to pray and make dua - not only because you want something, but because you have a lot to be thankful for too.

Task: Now is the perfect time for reflection. What are you grateful for?

ALHAMDULLILAH FOR...

Prophet Musa (AS)

Day eighteen

Allah (SWT) loved Prophet Musa (AS) so much that He mentioned him more than ANY other prophet in the Quran. Allah (SWT) even SPOKE directly to Prophet Musa (AS)! That's probably why you might hear people call him 'Kalimullah' - The one with whom Allah (SWT) spoke.

Task: Pick up a book, ask a loved one or research the life of Prophet Musa (AS) online and share what you have learned with your family over your iftar meal.

PROPHET
MUSA
(AS)

The Night of Power

Do you know why the last ten nights of Ramadan are EXTRA important?

SURAH AL-QADR is dedicated to a very special night that reportedly falls on the last ten nights of Ramadan.

THAT NIGHT IS LAYLATUL QADR.

We aren't exactly sure which night it is, but what we do know is that it falls on an odd numbered night i.e 21st, 23rd, 25th, 27th or 29th.

It is the most BLESSED NIGHT in the whole, entire year.

Did you know that Allah (SWT) revealed the Quran to Prophet Muhammad (SAW) for the very first time on THIS night?

THAT'S EQUIVALENT TO 83 YEARS!

Allah (SWT) says so in Surah Al-Qadr. He (SWT) tells us that this night is BETTER than ONE THOUSAND months of worship.

Can you believe it?

Right up until sunrise, angels descend on to earth in their MILLIONS, probably even BILLIONS! That's how much of a big deal Laylatul Qadr is. Even angel Jibreel is sent down by Allah (SWT) and he's ONLY ever sent down for special occasions.

So what can we do to get the reward of ONE THOUSAND months of worship? Well, because we can't be sure EXACTLY which day Laylatul Qadr will fall on, it's VERY important to make sure that we spend EVERY NIGHT in the last ten nights of Ramadan being the best version of ourselves.

HERE ARE A LIST OF THINGS YOU CAN DO ON LAYLATUL QADR:

1. Pray your daily salah on time.
2. Pray extra nafl prayers.
3. Read surahs directly from the Quran.
4. Make dua for your loved ones and the Muslim Ummah.
5. Give to a charity of your choice.

Day nineteen (cont)

Task: Fill in the gaps to complete the sentences.

1) The Night of Power is also called _____.

2) Surah _____ explores Laylatul Qadr in detail.

3) Laylatul Qadr reportedly falls on the _____ ten nights of Ramadan.

4) Laylatul Qadr is the most _____ night in the whole entire year.

5) It was on this night Allah (SWT) revealed the _____ to

_____.

6) Laylatul Qadr is better than _____ months of worship.

7) _____ come down to Earth in their millions.

8) You could pray extra _____ prayers and give money to _____.

9) You should pray your five daily _____ on time.

10) Try and made dua for your loved ones and the Muslim _____.

Al-Qadr	blessed	Laylatul Qadr
one thousand	salah	Ummah
nafl	angels	last
Quran	Prophet Muhammad (SAW)	charity

Laylatul Qadr

The reward for worshipping Allah (SWT) on LAYLATUL QADR is better than ONE THOUSAND MONTHS of worship.   THAT'S ROUGHLY 83 YEARS!

Alhamdullilah, how blessed we are that Allah (SWT) has made it so easy for us to be rewarded by Him.

Task: Create a checklist of ibadah (worship) that you can do on the last odd nights of Ramadan.

MY LAYLATUL QADR CHART

21st RAMADAN _____ ✓

23rd RAMADAN _____ ✓

25th RAMADAN _____ ✓

27th RAMADAN _____ ✓

29th RAMADAN _____ ✓

Day twenty one

GEOMETRIC PATTERNS are a very common type of Islamic Art.

They were extremely popular in early Islamic history and continue to be used ALL around the world. These BEAUTIFUL, intricate patterns are usually connecting and repeating lines that are often found painted on clothing, pottery and inside of mosques.

Task: Add your own touches to the geometric design below and then finish it off with a splash of colour.

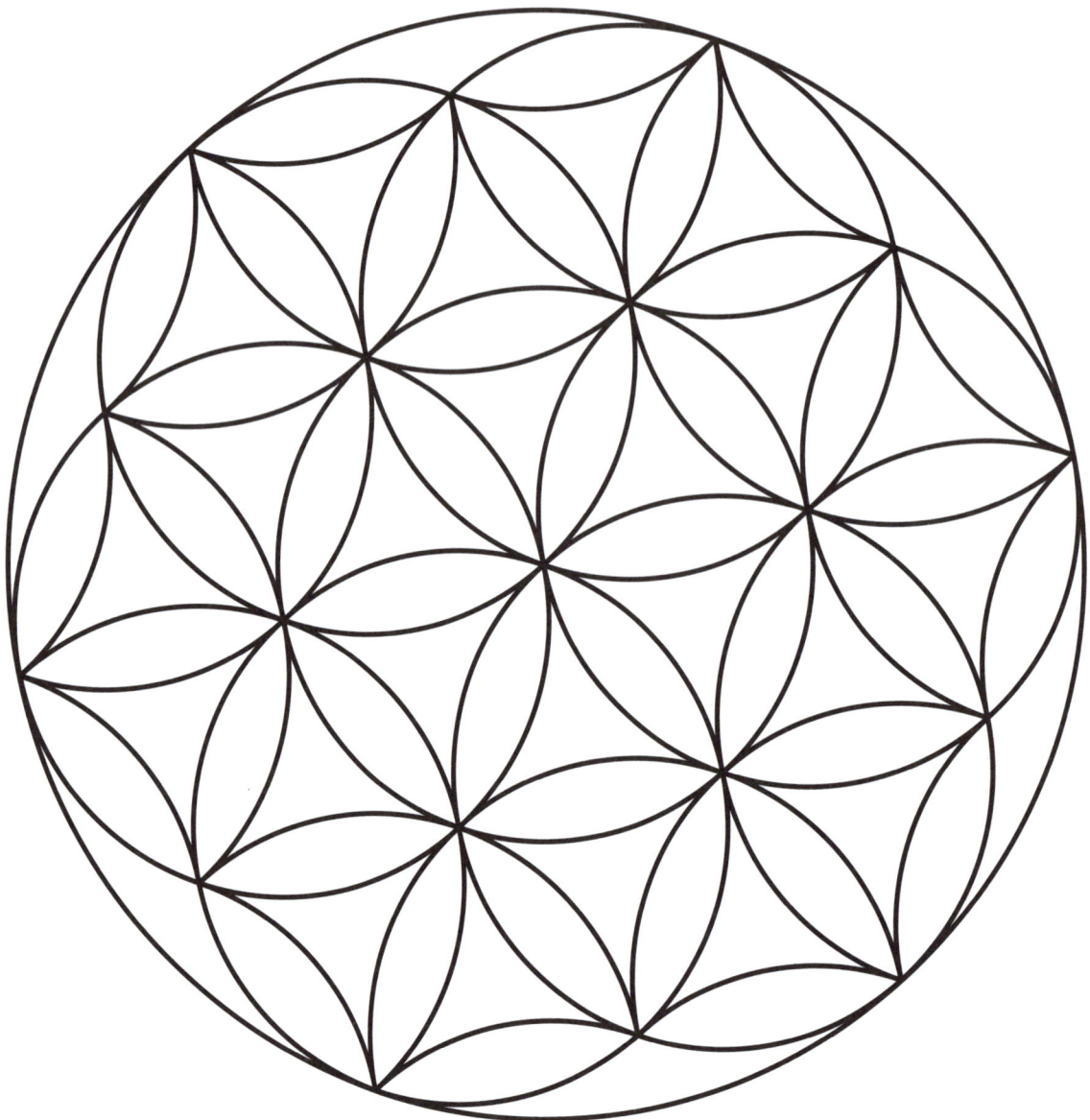

Day twenty two

Task: Put together a timetable to show a friend what a day during Ramadan looks like for you.

THINGS YOU COULD INCLUDE:

Waking up for suhoor, reading salah, doing dhikr, going for a walk, having an afternoon nap, preparing iftar etc.

TIMETABLE

TIME	ACTIVITY

Day twenty three

CIRCLE THE CORRECT ANSWER.

Don't worry if you find it tricky, have a really good guess and then use the answer page to check your work after. You may even learn something new and interesting that you can share with your family and friends!

1) WHICH PROPHET DID THE PEOPLE TRY TO CRUCIFY?

    a) Prophet Zakariyya (AS)   b) Prophet Yusuf (AS)   c) Prophet Isa (AS)

2) WHICH PROPHET IS ALSO KNOWN AS 'MAN OF THE FISH?'

    a) Prophet Yunus (AS)   b) Prophet Ayyub (AS)   c) Prophet Yaqub (AS)

3) HOW OLD WAS PROPHET MUHAMMAD (SAW) WHEN HE RECEIVED HIS FIRST REVELATION?

    a) 27   b) 33   c) 40

4) WHICH PROPHET'S NAME IS MENTIONED THE MOST IN THE QURAN?

    a) Prophet Yahya (AS)   b) Prophet Musa (AS)   c) Prophet Muhammad (SAW)

5) FOR HOW MANY YEARS DID PROPHET NUH (AS) PREACH TO HIS PEOPLE?

    a) 800 years   b) 950 years   c) 850 years

6) HOW WERE PROPHETS YAHYA AND ISA (AS) RELATED?

    a) They were siblings.   b) They were cousins.   c) They were uncle and nephew.

Day twenty four

RESEARCH the story of Prophet Ibrahim (AS), Hajar, their young son, Ismail (AS) and how the blessed water of Zam Zam came to be.

You can do your research by reading a book, asking a grown up or researching the story online.

Task: Retell the story in your own words. Don't forget to add lots of detail and description!

HOW ZAM ZAM CAME TO BE

Long, long ago, _____

_____

_____

_____

_____

_____

_____

_____

_____

_____

_____

Day twenty five

Task: Using what you already know, identify which statements about the Quran, seerah and sunnah are true and which ones are false.

STATEMENT

1) THE QURAN WAS REVEALED IN THE MONTH OF DHUL HIJJAH. ✓ ✗

2) 'AL FATIHAH' MEANS THE OPENING. ✓ ✗

3) AISHA (RA) WAS PROPHET MUHAMMAD'S (SAW) FIRST WIFE. ✓ ✗

4) THERE ARE EIGHT LEVELS OF HEAVEN. ✓ ✗

5) THE QIBLAH DIRECTION WAS ONCE TOWARDS JERUSALEM. ✓ ✗

6) THE QURAN WAS REVEALED OVER 23 YEARS. ✓ ✗

7) PROPHET ISA (AS) FIRST SPOKE AT THE AGE OF 2. ✓ ✗

8) PERFORMING UMRAH IN THE MONTH OF RAMADAN WILL RECEIVE THE SAME REWARD AS PERFORMING HAJJ. ✓ ✗

9) THERE IS A PIECE OF JANNAH ON EARTH. ✓ ✗

Day twenty six

AL SAKHRAH MOSQUE (Dome of the Rock) is often mistaken as AL AQSA MOSQUE. It's probably because they're so close to each other, right? The easiest way to remember which is which is that Al Aqsa has a grey dome and Al Sakhrah has a gold dome.

DID YOU KNOW?

Muslims used to pray towards Al Aqsa mosque until some time after Prophet Muhammad (SAW) migrated to Madinah. It was then Allah (SWT) commanded that the qibla direction change to face the direction of the Kabah.

Task: Have a go at replicating the designs on Al Sakhrah mosque.

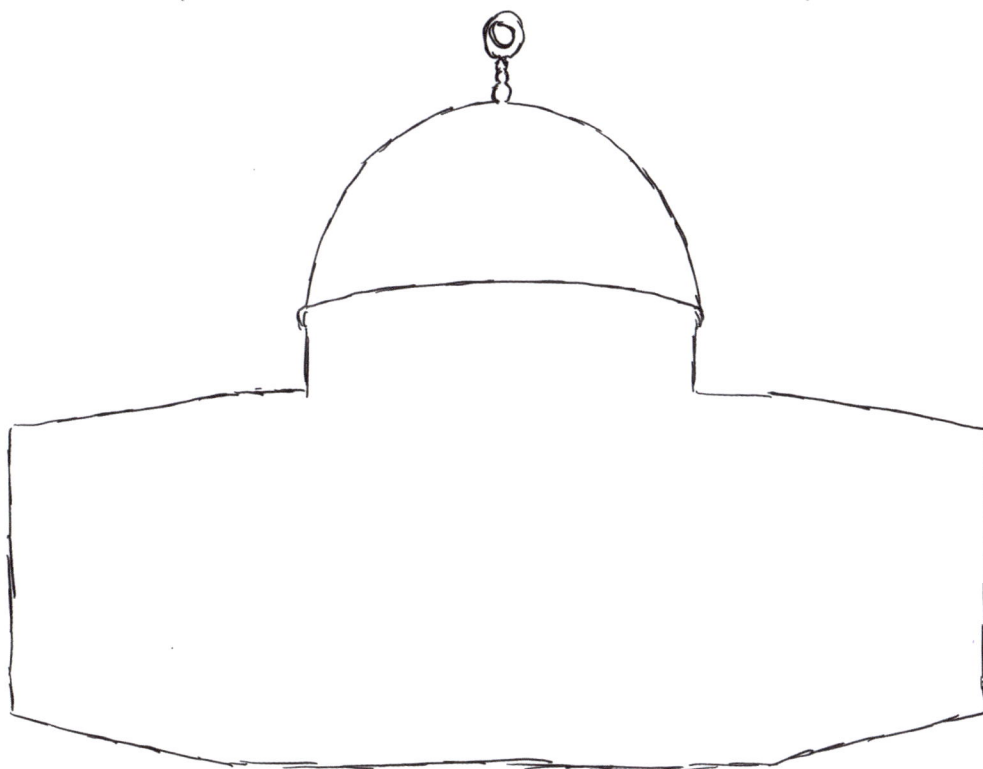

Day twenty seven

THE NIGHT JOURNEY - FROM MAKKAH TO JERUSALEM.

One night, Prophet Muhammad (SAW) went on a MIRACULOUS journey that eventually led him through the gates of JANNAH.

It all began when Angel Jibreel descended onto Earth and brought with him a lightning fast beast (al-Buraq) for Prophet Muhammad (SAW) to travel on. They rode through the night and stopped only to pray.

They stopped in the land of the date palms, they stopped on Mount Sinai, they stopped in Bethlehem and then they stopped once more. Prophet Muhammad (SAW) dismounted as they reached Masjid Al-Aqsa and was led inside by angel Jibreel.

IT WAS REPORTED that in that moment angel Jibreel called the adhan. It was in that moment that Prophet Muhammad (SAW) led ALL of the other 124,000 prophets in prayer. It was said that in that moment even the angels descended to pray behind the seal of the prophets.

Some time had passed and Prophet Muhammad (SAW) ascended up to the Heavens. THE ANGELS REJOICED! Prophet Muhammad (SAW) stood firm.

He stood in the first to the seventh. Prophet Muhammad (SAW) met Adam (AS), Isa (AS) and Yahya (AS). He met Yusuf (AS), Idris AS) and Harun (AS). He met Musa (AS) and Ibrahim (AS) until finally, Prophet Muhammad (SAW) met his Lord.

PROPHET MUHAMMAD (SAW) MET ALLAH (SWT).

It was then Allah (SWT) gave us our daily salah. It began with fifty and was reduced to five. However, the reward always remained the same.

Task: Try and remember the story and retell it to your loved ones.

Day twenty eight

Task: Do some research online and design your own Eid card. Try and make it EXTRA personal to show your loved one how important they are to you.

Day twenty nine

SENTENCE MAT

- Eid Mubarak!
- Have a blessed day!
- May your day be filled with goodness and barakah!
- Thank you for making this Ramadan...
- My favourite memory was...
- You made me smile when...
- Next year. I will...
- You are always in my duas.
- May He always keep us close. Ameen.

You did it!
ALHAMDULLILAH

You have completed your Thirty Days of Ramadan Activity Journal. We hope that you have learned a lot and reap the rewards of sharing your new learning with your loved ones. We pray that your Ramadan was filled with love, duas, blessings and mercy.

Your favourite activity:

Something new you have learned:

Something you have achieved this Ramadan:

Two things you would like to learn more about:

Your goals for next Ramadan:

Your favourite Ramadan memory:

May Allah (SWT) accept your ibadah, fasts and continue to guide you towards Him. Ameen.

MY TALEEM

MY THIRTY days OF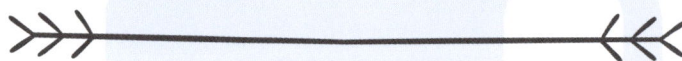 RAMADAN activity JOURNAL

ANSWER PAGES

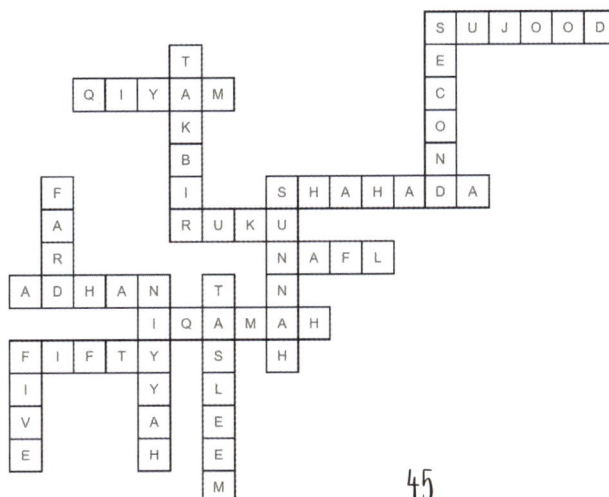

DAY TWO:

A) IN SHA ALLAH

B) SUBHAN'ALLAH

C) MA SHAA'ALLAH TABAARAK ALLAH

D) ASTAGFIRULLAH

E) FISABILLAH

DAY THREE:

M	A	D	A	R	T	N	D	P	A	S	D	F	I
U	E	A	X	Y	U	Y	U	S	U	F	G	S	B
H	W	H	G	I	O	K	W	H	J	H	A	H	R
A	L	Y	A	S	A	L	A	Z	X	C	V	U	A
M	Z	U	Y	Y	T	S	D	R	Y	N	B	A	H
M	A	I	S	U	L	A	Y	M	A	N	M	I	I
A	K	O	P	N	S	L	T	E	Q	W	Q	B	M
D	A	A	H	U	D	E	D	F	U	G	T	N	H
N	R	I	T	S	E	H	S	D	B	B	U	U	J
B	I	S	L	R	W	Q	Z	X	C	V	L	R	K
V	Y	M	Y	Y	A	H	Y	A	A	C	N	A	L
C	A	A	U	I	A	L	F	I	K	L	U	H	D
A	H	I	D	R	I	S	D	I	S	H	A	Q	M
I	O	L	E	E	M	U	S	A	B	A	Y	U	B

DAY FIVE:

A) AL QUDDUS - THE PURE

B) AL GHAFFAR - THE FORGIVER/THE FORGIVING

C) AL MU'MIN - THE GRANTER OF SECURITY

D) AL HAKEEM - THE WISE

E) AL KAREEM - THE GENEROUS/THE NOBLE

F) AL MUQEET - THE NOURISHER/THE SUSTAINER

G) AL HAFIZ - THE GUARDIAN

H) ASH SHAKUR - THE MOST APPRECIATIVE

I) AL ALIM -THE ALL KNOWING

J) AL WAHHAB - THE BESTOWER OF GIFTS

K) AS SABUR - THE PATIENT

DAY SEVEN:

1) ONE THOUSAND YEARS

2) IDOLS

3) HE WAS A BLESSED MAN WITH INCREDIBLE PATIENCE

4) BEAUTIFUL AND ELOQUENT

5) ANY FOUR FROM - SUN, MOON, SHIMMERING STARS, NIGHT SKY, MOUNTAINS, DESERTS, RIVERS, TREES, EVERYTHING THAT LIVES AND BREATHES.

6) TO WORK HARD TO ACHIEVE SOMETHING.

7) FALSE- HE DID WHAT WAS ASKED OF HIM AND NEVER QUESTIONED IT AS HE HAD FAITH IN ALLAH.

8) THE BELIEVERS WERE GRATEFUL AND TRUSTED IN ALLAH.

DAY NINE:

45

DAY TEN:
1) AL MALAIKAH
2) PURE LIGHT
3) DISOBEY ALLAH (SWT), COMMIT SIN OR READ QURAN
4) FALSE - ANGELS CAN TAKE THE FORM OF HUMANS
5) WE KNOW BECAUSE IT IS IN THE QURAN OR FROM THE SUNNAH
6) FALSE - ANGELS GATHER AND LISTEN TO US RECITE QURAN BECAUSE THEY CAN NOT READ IT THEMSELVES
7) ACCEPT ANY ANSWER FROM THE TEXT

ANGEL MUNKAR & NAKEER	These angels question the souls in the grave.
ANGEL RAQIB & ATID	These angels are the scribes and record your good and bad deeds.
ANGEL RIDHWAN	He guards the gates of Jannah.
ANGEL MIKAIL	He is in charge of rainfall and waters the land.
ANGEL JIBREEL	This angel receives Allah's (SWT) words and tells them to the prophets.
ANGEL ISRAFEEL	He is in charge of blowing the trumpet on Judgement Day

DAY ELEVEN:
SURAH AN-NISA -THE WOMEN - 4
SURAH AL-NAHL -THE BEE - 16
SURAH AL-KAHF -THE CAVE - 18
SURAH AL-ANBIYA -THE PROPHETS - 21
SURAH AL-NUR -THE LIGHT - 24
SURAH AL-ANKABUT -THE SPIDER - 29
SURAH AL-NAJM -THE STAR - 53
SURAH AL-LAYL-THE NIGHT - 92
SURAH AL-FIL-THE ELEPHANT - 105
SURAH AL-NASR-THE HELP - 110
SURAH AL-FALAQ-THE DAYBREAK - 113

DAY TWELVE:

DAY THIRTEEN:
IBRAHIM
FATIMA
ZAINAB
QASIM
AISHA
HAFSA
KHADIJAH
AMINA
ABDULLAH

1) KHADIJAH
2) ABUDLLAH
3) ZAINAB
4) MARIYAH
5) PATERNAL GRANDFATHER
6) AMINA
7) QASIM
8) SIX

DAY FOURTEEN:
1) SALAH
2) BISMILLAH
3) HAJJ
4) QURAN
5) MUHAMMAD (SAW)
6) SHAWWAL
7) SUHOOR
8) TARAWEEH
9) LAYLATUL QADR
10) SUNNAH

DAY TWENTY THREE
1) C
2) A
3) C
4) B
5) B
6) B

DAY TWENTY FIVE
1) FALSE. THE QURAN WAS REVEALED IN THE MONTH OF RAMADAN.
2) TRUE.
3) FALSE. KHADIJAH (RA) WAS THE FIRST WIFE OF PROPHET MUHAMMAD (SAW).
4) FALSE. THERE ARE SEVEN LEVELS OF HEAVEN.
5) TRUE.
6) TRUE.
7) FALSE. PROPHET ISA (AS) SPOKE AT BIRTH.
8) TRUE.
9) TRUE.

DAY SIXTEEN
I AM AS MY SERVANT THINKS OF ME.
CALL UPON ME I WILL RESPOND TO YOU.
DO GOOD AND GOOD WILL COME TO YOU.
EVERY ACT OF GOODNESS IS SADAQAH.

DAY NINETEEN
1) LAYLATUL QADR
2) AL-QADR
3) LAST
4) BLESSED
5) QURAN/PROPHET MUHAMMAD (SAW)
6) ONE THOUSAND
7) ANGELS
8) NAFL/CHARITY
9) SALAH
10) UMMAH